BE SAFE ON THE INTERNET

BRIDGET HEOS   ILLUSTRATED BY SILVIA BARONCELLI

Amicus Illustrated is published by Amicus
P.O. Box 1329, Mankato, MN 56002
www.amicuspublishing.us

Library of Congress Cataloging-in-Publication Data
Heos, Bridget.
  Be safe on the Internet / Bridget Heos ; illustrated by Silvia Baroncelli.
      pages cm. — (Be safe!)
  Includes bibliographical references.
  Summary: "A young boy named Aidan teaches his curious puppy how to stay safe online"— Provided by publisher.
  Audience: Grade K to 3.
  ISBN 978-1-60753-445-7 (library binding) —
ISBN 978-1-60753-660-4 (ebook)
  1. Internet and children—Juvenile literature. 2. Computer crimes—Prevention—Juvenile literature. 3. Online etiquette—Juvenile literature. I. Baroncelli, Silvia, illustrator. II. Title.
  HQ784.I58H44 2015   JNF
  004.67'80832—dc23   004.67   2013032364
                                           HEOS

Editor: Rebecca Glaser
Designer: Kathleen Petelinsek

Printed in the United States of America,
at Corporate Graphics in North Mankato, Minn.
10 9 8 7 6 5 4 3

ABOUT THE AUTHOR

Bridget Heos is the author of more than 60 children's books, including many advice and how-to titles. She lives safely in Kansas City with her husband and four children. You can find out more about her at www.authorbridgetheos.com.

ABOUT THE ILLUSTRATOR

Silvia Baroncelli has loved to draw since she was a child. She collaborates regularly with publishers in drawing and graphic design from her home in Prato, Italy. Her best collaborators are her four nephews, daughter Ginevra, and organized husband Tommaso. Find out more about her on the web at silviabaroncelli.it

Oh, hey Buddy. You want to play?

4

I *guess* I could teach you.
First of all, you're just a puppy,
so only go on kid-friendly websites.

That game is too violent.

Ask a grown-up which sites you can go on. My mom lets me play on this site. You need to create an account.

And don't use *my* real name either. Make up a screen name, like Bacon Fan 2000. Now you need a password.

That's too easy. Choose a password
that would be hard for others to guess.

Who are you calling?

Don't call your friends and tell them your password! It's private. You should only tell Mom and Dad.

Choose a new password. Now you can play games on this website.

What if you want to look up information on the Web? That's a good search.

But don't buy anything on the Internet, okay? Only a grown-up should order things online.

Let's say you want to set up an e-mail account. That way you can e-mail friends and family. The same rules apply. Create a username and password.

You should let Mom check your e-mails.
If you get an e-mail from a stranger, or a
mean e-mail, she can take care of it.

Sorry, that e-mail is fake. You didn't really win a million bacon treats. E-mails like this are called spam.

Never give away personal information like your address, phone number, or school name. And don't reply to strangers.

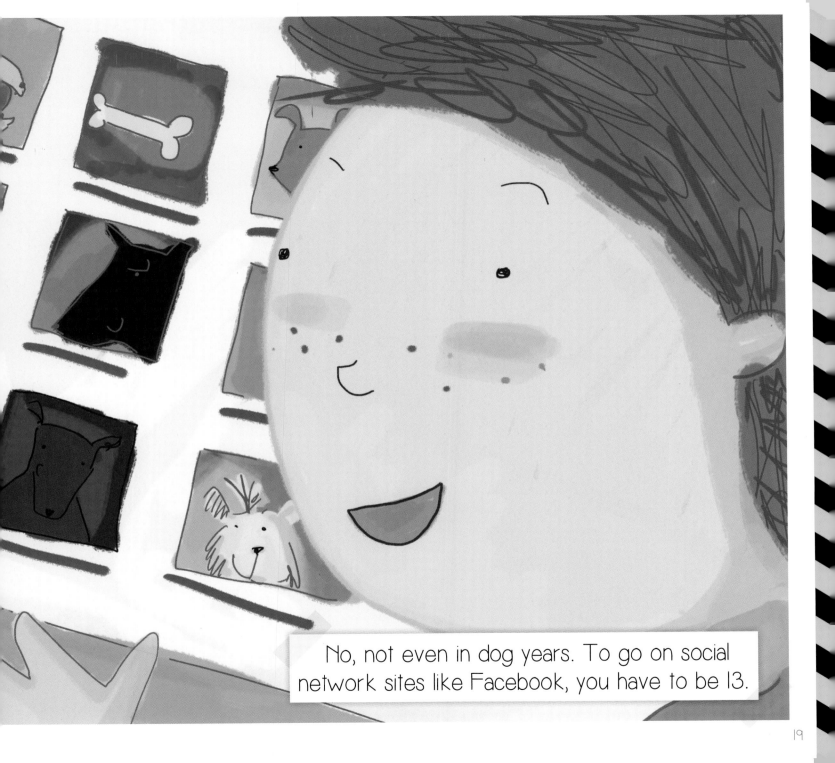

No, not even in dog years. To go on social network sites like Facebook, you have to be 13.

No matter where you are on the Internet, be nice.

That's mean, Buddy. Even if you're just joking, you can get in trouble for being mean on the Internet. You could also hurt someone's feelings. I think we need a break.

RULES TO REMEMBER: INTERNET SAFETY

- Don't give out your real name, address, phone number, or school name.
- Keep your passwords private.
- Don't buy things on the Internet.
- Ask a parent before visiting a new website.
- Don't visit chat rooms.
- Tell a parent if you get an e-mail from someone you don't know. Don't reply to the e-mail.
- Tell a parent if someone is being mean or acting strangely on the Internet.
- Be nice.

GLOSSARY WORDS

account A collection of the information you enter and your activity on a particular website.

Internet A system of websites that connects computers around the world.

password A word that lets you log in to an Internet account.

screen name A name a person chooses to represent himself or herself online, so that their real name is kept private.

social network An online service that allows a person to make a profile about themselves, post updates, and connect with friends and family.

spam E-mail sent by a stranger to sell something or steal information.

website A group of Web pages created by a person, business, school, or organization for the public.

READ MORE

Herrington, Lisa M. *Internet Safety*. New York: Children's Press, 2013.

Lee, Sally. *Staying Safe Online*. Mankato, Minn.: Capstone Press, 2012.

Rooney, Anne. *Internet Safety*. Mankato, Minn.: Sea-to-Sea Publications, 2013.

Spivet, Bonnie. *Stopping Cyberbullying*. New York: PowerKids Press, 2012.

WEBSITES

FBI— KIDS SAFETY
http://www.fbi.gov/fun-games/kids/kids-safety
Learn about Internet safety from the FBI.

NETSMARTZKIDS HOME PAGE
http://www.netsmartzkids.org/
Watch videos and read eBooks to learn how to be safe online.

WEBONAUTS INTERNET ACADEMY I PBS KIDS GO!
http://pbskids.org/webonauts/
Go through a Webonaut training game to learn about acting responsibly on the Internet.